D1271813

CAREFULNESS

by Janet Riehecky
illustrated by Kathryn Hutton

THE CHILD'S WORLD

Mankato, MN 56001

Three little kittens lost their mittens,
And they began to cry,
"Oh, mother dear,
We sadly fear,
Our mittens we have lost."

"What? Lost your mittens?
You naughty kittens!
Then you shall have no pie."
"Meow! Meow!"
"No, you shall have no pie."

The three little kittens, they found their mittens,
And they began to cry,
"Oh, mother dear,
See here. See here.
Our mittens we have found."

"What? Found your mittens?
You good little kittens!
Then you can have some pie."
"Purr-r! Purr-r!"
"Yes, you can have some pie."

—Mother Goose

Library of Congress Cataloging in Publication Data

Riehecky, Janet, 1953-
     Carefulness / by Janet Riehecky ; illustrated by Kathryn Hutton.
         p. cm. — (Values to live by)
     Summary: Defines carefulness by presenting situations in which it
is important to be careful.
     ISBN 0-89565-564-0
     1. Children's accidents—Prevention—Juvenile literature.
[1. Safety.   2. Conduct of life.]   I. Hutton, Kathryn, ill.
II. Title.   III. Series.
HV675.5.R54   1990
613.6—dc20   89-71195
                                                         CIP
                                                          AC

What is carefulness? Carefulness is keeping track of your mittens so they don't get lost.

Carefulness is making sure you don't
spill soup in your lap.

And when you have your new shoes
on, carefulness is waiting to play in
the puddles.

When you scrub the bottoms *and* the
tops of your hands before dinner,
that's carefulness.

Making your bed so there are hardly
any wrinkles is carefulness . . .

and so is putting your toys on the shelf
so they won't fall off.

When you do your work at school,
carefulness is listening to the teacher's
instructions, . . .

thinking about the answer, . . .

and making sure you write *all* the
letters in your name.

Carefulness is looking both ways
before you cross a street . . .

and slowing down when you ride your
bike past someone.

Making sure the slide is clear before
you go down is carefulness.

And looking before you throw
the Frisbee is carefulness too.

When you do the dishes, carefulness
is handling them gently and getting
them completely dry before you put
them away.

Carefulness is pulling weeds—not
flowers—when you help your mother
in the garden.

When you check to be sure it's clear
before you jump in the water, that's
carefulness.

And when you hand scissors to a friend point down, that's carefulness too.

Carefulness is putting away your
toys so your little sister can't get
them . . .

and it's giving her a gentle hug instead
of a tackle.

Carefulness is making sure none of
your toys are left out . . .

and carefulness is turning out the light
when you leave a room.

Carefulness is paying close attention to
what you're doing. It's taking the time
to do it right. When you're careful,
you avoid accidents and you do your
best work.